BOY
WITH
THORN

PITT POETRY SERIES

Ed Ochester, Editor

BOY
WITH
THORN

RICKEY LAURENTIIS

UNIVERSITY OF PITTSBURGH PRESS

This book is the winner of the 2014 Cave Canem Poetry Prize, selected by Terrance Hayes.

Founded in 1996 by poets Toi Derricotte and Cornelius Eady, Cave Canem is a home for the many voices of African American poetry and is committed to cultivating the artistic and professional growth of African American poets.

Established in 1999, the Cave Canem Poetry Prize is awarded annually to an exceptional manuscript by an African American poet who has not yet published a full-length book of poems.

Support for the Cave Canem Poetry Prize has been provided, in part, from The Ford Foundation, Lannan Foundation, and individual donors.

ART WORKS.
arts.gov

Published by the University of Pittsburgh Press, Pittsburgh, Pa., 15260
Copyright © 2015, Rickey Laurentiis
All rights reserved
Manufactured in the United States of America
Printed on acid-free paper
10 9 8 7 6 5 4
ISBN 13: 978-0-8229-6381-3
ISBN 10: 0-8229-6381-7

CONTENTS

◆

◆

FOREWORD

TERRANCE HAYES

Reading Rickey Laurentiis's *Boy with Thorn*, I recalled something Philip Levine said about Mark Doty's *My Alexandria* more than twenty years ago: "If it were mine to invent a poet to complete the century of William Carlos Williams and Wallace Stevens, I would create Mark Doty just as he is." A similar pronouncement seems appropriate here. Except the astonishing poetry of Rickey Laurentiis feels not like the completion of a century but the opening of a brilliant new door in poetry's enduring shelter.

The poetic lair (and lure) of Laurentiis, I'd say, recalls Frank Loyd Wright's Fallingwater house, a stone home built on moving water. This poetry is fluid and assured. It integrates interior and exterior worlds, demotic and eccentric idioms, swagger and humility. One senses the poets who have informed Rickey Laurentiis, but their influence seems more telepathic (subtle) than telegraphed (advertised). There is a restlessness to this book that recalls James Baldwin as well as W. H. Auden, for example, and an integrity that recalls Audre Lorde as well as Robert Hayden. We see, not incidentally, Wallace Stevens in the sublime "Of the Leaves That Have Fallen," a poem that is both homage and critique: "Like Wallace Stevens, I know the dark is crucial. / I sing, I grieve in it, I dream what haunts each night: / These bodies, even lynched, still are thinking." *Boy with Thorn* has the intensity of a Stevens who is a disciple of water (engrossing and immersive) rather than snow (cool and detached). "Like you, I was born underwater," Laurentiis writes in "Epitaph on a Stone." "I am the man / stepping up to the water," he writes in "Mood for Love." His fluid, fluent style gives this mature debut a thoroughness and, more intriguingly, a curiosity that is beguiling, supple, and discerning: "I watched him, silent, beside me, take / the rotten earth into his mouth, and / sober, with little shame, chew . . ." (from "Carnal Knowledge"). The poems can feel wonderfully feline as they manage to be discrete while exuding palpable intimacies. Sometimes it is the enraptured, sprawling intimacy of "Little Song":

> Given what I am,   if
> not cannibal for, animal for: he
>   who let go a door in me, be-
> cracked my sternum to a hundred flashing moths, oh handsome, oh—Truth
>   be told: I hungered this, needled it out, I
>   stretched for this.

Sometimes it is the piquant, punctuated intimacy of "Quiet Please":

> And so it was. Violation.
> Betrayal. What is it but the ego
> brought out, invited, into the best possible
> light—defined by it—until blinded?
> I'm speaking of a wounding.

Call Rickey Laurentiis's stylistic range *virtuosity* or call it, just as correctly, *necessity*—a range essential to the protean lives these poems praise, elegize, and shelter. It is important to note the remarkable ways the poems are embodying those lives as much as they are singing and thinking of them. Laurentiis's use of language mirrors the complexities of sexuality, race, and spirituality. The observations that characterize typical ekphrastic poetry, for example, are elevated to witness (especially the traumas and politics of witness) in poems like "Black Iris," "Vanitas with Negro Boy," and "Study in Black." In "I Saw I Dreamt Two Men" Laurentiis writes of two men "hoisted, hung up . . . Their black skin made blacker by my feeding." The poem's stunned and stunning final couplet ("As I saw the other turn away apart stay with silence / I stayed with southern silence") mirrors the feel of "southern silence." Through it and so many of the poems here I understand "southern" ("Conditions for a Southern Gothic," "Southern Gothic," "A Southern Wind") as a refrain for a landscape that is simultaneously seductive and destructive; a pastoral past that is mutually murderous and magical. Rickey Laurentiis navigates language and history with his "American tongue" and "crucial blood," his "hauntedness" and "stubbornness," and, most especially, the extraordinary force of his grace.

"You have seen what happens when a stone / plops onto the tension of the water—it moves / through the water, or the water moves away from it," he writes in "Modern Ripple." This amazing debut is a refuge as open and irrepressible as water, as resolute and penetrating as stone.

And ghosts must do again
What gives them pain.

W. H. AUDEN

Conditions for a Southern Gothic

Therefore, my head was kingless.
I was a head alone, moaning in a wet black field.
    I was like any of those deserter slaves
whose graves are just the pikes raised for their heads, reshackled, blue
    and plain as fear.
All night I whistled at a sky that mocked me,
that fluently changed its grammar as if to match desire in my eye.
    My freedom is possible, it said.
As if my torn-off head in that bed swamped and whelming then
with water had one wish, and it did: to think stranger stuff,
to break that boring need to always have a shadow trail its maker, such that:
1. The shadow snaps, rising to kiss the head;
2. The kiss lands, the head flies up in airy revolt;
3. Cracked from the head come the crows of its thinking;
4. Three crows move in minstrelsy against the night;
5. And the head still singing: *Last night, a Negro was axed . . .*

Who among us was made to scratch a myth? Speak.
If God made us in his image, it was the first failure of the imagination.

I Saw I Dreamt Two Men

I saw I dreamt

Two men hoisted hung up not American the rope
Not closed on their breathing

But this rope tied them spine to spine somehow

Suspended
From the mood of a tree not American they were

African Ugandan Nigerian

Without a license a right to touch
The sin their touching incites

And I heard their names called out *Revision*

Or Die and *You Must Repent*
And *Forget the Lie you Lily-Boys you Faggots*

Called up from the mob

Of their mothers their fathers
With Christ in the blood who had Christ in the blood

Who sung out "Abide with Me"

This was my eyes' closed-eyed vision
This is what a darkness makes

And how did I move from that distance to intimacy

So close I could see
The four soles of their feet so close I was kneeled

Could lick

Those feet as if I was because I became
The fire who abided

I saw that I dreamt

Their black skin made blacker by my feeding
I thought Christ

Why did I think

Their black skin tipped blacker by this American
Feeding but just one shot up

A cry African it was

American *O Lord abide with me*
It was human lusty flat

You had to be in the hollow of it to taste it

You had to see how in such lack
Invention takes hold

They say some dreams come in the moment

Of waking
Stitched because daylight likes a story

That some dreams are extensions

Of an itch
Thief-walking the coral of the brain

I say

But I did feel that one blue mouth blow out
As I felt

The mood of that tree

As I saw the other turn away apart stay with silence
I stayed with southern silence

One Country

I want to be released from it.
I want its impulses stunned to lead.
This body. Its breath.
Let it. Let the whole pageant
end. If my body had a river in it
I would drain it. If by the river
was a city, let a storm shock and drown it.
If in the city was a boy made sick
from his body, the freak passions of it,
let him come out—his brown skin
lifting as a shell. Let it. Let all
his limbs pop and unhinge. First
his penis, its quick flight, as if a comet.
The eight fingers next, then thumbs,
then tongue, till every star is on the floor,
dismissed, each pointing in its own
direction, each another door
to the one country where his body is
loved and made for.

Black Iris

Georgia O'Keeffe, early twentieth century, oil on canvas

Dark, imposing flesh. Darker still
its center, like the tongue of
a cow that has for a week now been
dead, spent during calf birth, and the calf
still clinging to her, and his own tongue
wild for want of milk, and the calf
with flies in his eyes—*that* color: near-to-
purple, bruised. I should call it
beautiful, or beauty itself, this dark
room, broom closet, this nigger-dot.
I should want to fit into it, stand up in it,
rest, as would any beast inside a stable.
I should want to own it, force it mine,
to know it is my nature, and of
course don't I? Why shouldn't I want?

Black mirror. Space delicate
and cracked. Now anything could
go in there: a fist, veined, fat.
A body. And here runs the blood
through the body, deep, watery.
And here runs the message in the blood:
This is it—fuck her fag like you're supposed to.
And when the wind shakes

9

and when the iris shakes in it,
the lips of the flower shaping
to the thing that invades it, that will be
me, there, shaking, my voice shaking,
like the legs of the calf, who—out of fear?
out of duty?—is sitting by his dead
mother because what else will he do, what else has he?
Because a voice outside him makes him.

Lord and Chariot

I say the dead done caught me in a special knot
    and lured, and dragged me to the interior.
I say his face is strange here, a moment cruel
    but not without its silk, its earned sadness.
He asks me to touch it, so I touch it. No light
    can blossom here I know, as my bones know.

      ◆

Why ask me who I am. Who really knows
    the place of my future? I'm his, or I'm not—
I'm black, or black was made me. The light
    turns the cane a wanted color. I walk its interior.
There are only grasses here, only sadness.
    I pick one. I tear it. I think to be free is to be cruel.

      ◆

He says the dead are versions of himself: little ulcers,
    little cruel insurgencies. He says, Know
that I'm master here, my boy, my little sadness.
    There is no riot. (*Riot.*) Or fear. (*Fear.*) Bought, knotted,
I'm the boy in the cane field that's his, the air, or
    I'm his whip that stirred the air, scarred the light.

      ◆

My back is the touch of violence.   Like light,
      my blood trills.   I kneel.   I ooze.   Cruel
underworld, I freeze in your interior—
      Though I'm called queen.   I lie at his waist.   I know
the true color of his loved-on skin.   I say it's white, not
      purity.   I say that my strength is my sadness.

                    ◆

To be free, I think, like him, is a sadness—
      Nothing at all.   But to be bold, to light
a panic, to tear a cage of cane by blade is not
      freedom, either.   The cane grows back.   *Cruel*—
Can't you see it's the one word I know?   Even my bones know
      this language, and moan it deep in their interior.

                    ◆

I say the dead done left me, stranded, at the interior,
      which is this stranger's face, his sprawling sadness.
I say any blade in my hand is just my hand, and I know
      its weight exactly, the lift of its bite.   O light:
sweet molestation in the fields.   One lord.   One chariot.   Cruel
      silk, I'm a boy in love.   Let the dead bury their dead.

Ghazal for Emmett Till

Quiet now your tongue You're in this cotton land
Oaks swing long limbs of men on this cotton land

You come with song stuck under your heels as heat
The moist pinprick of flesh Jazz of this tin land

You come with language of the sharp-jawed breath
Snow How it pops beneath the eyelids within land

You come They won't have your sin Your cocked fedora
Can't mask your grin much longer on this rotten land

You come They will have your skin Your mettle
Your sole will leave the firmness of this whitened land

Quiet now your tongue You're spilling in the river's hand
Oaks cloud the sinking of your finger in this cotton land

Carnal Knowledge

I watched him, silent, beside me, take
the rotten earth into his mouth, and
sober, with little shame, chew . . .
In that altar between the gums of his teeth and his
teeth, he worked the many tired leaves
of it, downed, until it went ghost, not a thing
at all really—or only liquid now: earth
streaming from his lips, redone in bright
terrible braids, pairs of them, and spat
into a jar that could've been like prayer itself:
how faith can be that one container, bare-breasted,
which holds. I watched him, growing out
to the heat of it, like a root. And though I figure
this has something to do with power, I ignore it,
for once being the thing that only looks *at*—
eyes open, mouth ready, pregnant with the burn.

Mood Indigo

How is it out? Is, from the sky,
water still coming?

Are trees out? Do you hear
their argument? Do you know

it for an argument: how to manage
(*they are yelling*) this weather?

Where are birds? Why are they made
clairvoyant—flitting off, fluttering

like leaves on a single branch: they know
to evacuate, to separate from the living

world, about to be changed, world,
and the trees—?

2.

Though I cannot see you
still I know it is

you: man with the hard
kiss, the touch of Scorpion in his blood.

That means life for you is absolute.
There is either hunger

or no hunger. There is either *a body pleased*—.
Listen, the radio's dim utterance: *You*

ain't been blue, no, no . . . The sole
utterance. To move, in this dark house,

aimless—is that an utterance? Dinner
eaten, the dishes slowly washed: ignorance

or utterance? The weather outside,
weather, and the trees—.

3.

They are still trees, right, slamming the roof tiles?
They are trees—the world not yet totally remade?

4.

There is either *a body pleased*—
or no body. Creation

or there's violence. How are they out?
Not palmetto. I mean, oak. I mean, magnolia.

Aren't they lonely? Don't they feel
somehow cheated, somehow violated? *Here*

is my body for you to use and also to protect—that
was their contract with the birds, who are

gone, who didn't tell us they were gone.
Are you listening? Can you tell me where they went?

Of their solitude. How they share it.
How to be that alone

(*Here is my body, Scorpio, won't you top it?*)
—to be together and alone.

5.

Is the body responsive?—your question.
But don't you feel me? My body's tremor?

My legs? My back-in-an-arch? Each trembling as if
each the alcove for where the birds go?

6.

Splinters are not trees. Trees are not
flesh. Here is the scene:

Two men. Blacked out. Half-embracing.
As, from the sky, falls the still-coming water.

Life is absolute. There is either danger
in this house or there is love. Either warning

in the radio's voice (*your arrogance will not
protect you*) or there is love. Where are the gods

now, prophecy in a hard beak? Let them say:
Your body won't be spared. Let them say: *Your life*

is not recyclable like some trees.

Swing Low

We aren't the solid men.
  We bend like the number seven.
Dig at corners, eat cobwebs, we
  are barefoot and bare-legged.
  We hang like green in autumn.

We aren't the stolid men.
  We scribble in familiar ink
about sunfalls and night. We
  see the white in the sky, and sigh.
  We lie with penciled grins.

We aren't the men, any men.
  We rip at the neck and wonder why
while rattlers roll in. Bent
  as a number, crooked, sundered,
  we aren't the idle lightning

if black thunder.

Vanitas with Negro Boy

David Bailly, seventeenth century, oil on canvas

I'll show you a bone made to hold on to.
A pip. A dense fire in which once
the thinking imagination sprawled
like a breathing vine. He would put the skull
on the table (*And nearest to the worn
flowers, sir, or nearer to the flute?*) turned
just so so not to be too crude. That
was the boy's job, this cage with a debt
in it (*And whose boy am I, and what is
my name?*). Black erasing blackness,
body and backdrop: you are not permitted to enter
the question light asks of his skin as if it were
a field, a mind, a word inclined to be
entered. It's true: his face, his boyhood even
(*And what is my boyhood, and where is it from?*)
would fade if not for the rope of attention
yanked glittering across that face. Look.
This is my painting, my version of the Dutch
stilleven. I'm trying to write obsession
into it, and can. Open your eyes. Don't run.
Vanitas, from the Latin for "emptiness,"
"meaningless"—but what nothing can exist
if thought does, if the drawn likeness of a bone
still exists? Why trust the Old Masters? Old

Masters, never trust me. Listen: each day
is a Negro boy, chained, slogging out of the waves,
panting, gripping the sum of his captain, the head,
ripped off, the blood purpling down, the red
hair flossed between the knuckles, swinging it
before him like judgment, saying to the mist,
then not, then quietly only to himself, *This is what
I'll do to you, what you dream I do, sir, if you like it.*

King of Shade, King of Scorpions

Then it was cold, like small and selfish
teeth, then it was rude, like a poison, and that
was your voice, wasn't it, and that
was the thrust of your voice taking up my own,
as any boy takes up his kite, in the village,
in the sheep-ring he manages, as the god that will
swoop down and take him. Weren't these the days
of abduction, after all, not rape? When to prove
your devotion insisted a theft of some kind: tear way
the boy-flesh, the boy-bone, and there it is:
the solid, red muscle, the thrush, thrumming in its strict
and freakish shade. To know it, you had to
claim it; claim it, break it. The god penetrated,
with his raw antenna. You moved in me, like prayer.

Full

We made a crank, a clear
cry of rock against metal,

and the scent of six lit
bodies, their heads

low inside their caving chests.
When you curved into that first

heavy punch and cleaved
the white of my spine, I couldn't

know the spicy charm of it,
how you would arch my back

into the sad sickle of a moon,
or how the grain

of your tackle was *Dear lord*—

Little Song

Given what I am,   if
not cannibal for, animal for: he
            who let go a door in me, be-
cracked my sternum to a hundred flashing moths, oh handsome, oh—Truth
            be told: I hungered this, needled it out, I
stretched for this.   Always a field stirs, would
                stir, for want of being filled.   Dwell
of me, my Eden, my Hook.   In
                    pleasure weren't we founded?   At the
            start didn't we blend and blur?   I would be his bravery, illusion
of his fearlessness and his fear.   Given what I am   only,   of
meat: cut fire: the inconsolable: of these, *Him.*

Writing an Elegy

But so tangled in the branches they had to leave it, the conquistador's
black beard cut from his head whose neck had snapped,
his deadness the others had to burn then, for the wind to take evenly away.
If not for his lust, his sickness to chase, to claim her;
if not for that Native woman's quick intelligence, out-climbing . . .

This is what I see: the Spanish moss
as convicted to its branches—gray, colonial,
but in my century now, suspended so close each vein might well be a whole,
hanging
fiction of my mind. The moss
is a fiction of my mind: a screen, swinging
on its gothic hinges, making the light fussier as it swags, giving not just the trees
but my idea of them a Medusa look. That man,

I think, had wanted to feed something in himself
not worth feeding, had founded a world on it—
What is it
my mind wants to get at, always extending, hungering, looking
back, always tearing open again its own modernity,
as if each thought is more than the little present
moment it sounds like, but, raised at an angle, piercing me, having me imagine,
to build such antique violences in my head, it is a thorn? This moss
has been growing for ages now, can do nothing

but snag and grow. . . . What is it the mind won't
unsee, beautiful flaw? In another version, the woman dies
and her husband
braids her hair
through the trees.

He who Refuses Does Not Repent

Lashing, spilling forth, it therefore turns,
as do the lovers, their violence done, turn
into themselves, to the night—impregnable—alone—
just until one mouth speaks out *Who told you
you could do this to me? Who told you I need love?*
and he's shaking then, like the skinned, forced
into ragged armor—a kind of heart—a kind of heretic.
The other doesn't move, classically, his wings in rare position.

Quiet Please

And so it was. Violation.
Betrayal. What is it but the ego
brought out, invited, into the best possible
light—defined by it—until blinded?
I'm speaking of a wounding.
Internal. Of the moment the wound is
confirmed. Vision. Feeling. *Don't.*
Sounds of struggle. *Don't apologize.*
Sounds of the throat opening. Any species
of animals that rise, that vow to, even
after the first bullet, a second; even without
ever knowing what a "vow" is. *Don't*
try. Don't touch me now. And so
it was. Release. Aperture. The ego becomes
a harsh liquor. Then the ego
becomes, simply, a body's want for it.

Modern Ripple

You have seen what happens when a stone
plops onto the tension of the water—
                                        it moves
through the water, or the water moves away from it.

    This is immigrant, says water's movement
that purls, as is custom, that circuits like a fish.
                                        And what is a stone?
Is it a thought, an indurate wish—or faith? What if we

    were stone? What happens then—if we fell into the water's lap,
were felled like two branches, too heavy once they linked?
                                        (*Here we are:*

    two men in a river.) Will the water endure us
or sink?

Southern Gothic

About the dead having available to them
all breeds of knowledge,
some pure, others wicked, especially what is
future, and the history that remains
once the waters recede, revealing the land
that couldn't reject or contain it, and the land
that is not new, is indigo, is ancient, lived
as all the trees that fit and clothe it are lived,
simple pine, oak, grand magnolia, he said
they frighten him, that what they hold in their silences
silences: sometimes a boy will slip
from his climbing, drown but the myth knows why,
sometimes a boy will swing with the leaves.

Of the Leaves That Have Fallen

Wallace Stevens, "Like Decorations in a Nigger Cemetery"

1.

In the imagination there is no daylight and,
Like Wallace Stevens, I know the dark is crucial.
I sing, I grieve in it, I dream what haunts each night:
These bodies, even lynched, still are thinking.
Nothing is final, I'm told. *No man shall see the end—*
But them, my fathers, lifted into fire, like tongues.

2.

To navigate the dark you must listen, you must listen
To the dark: the wind, a wind in the trees, the birds,
Birds shaping a sound around the green busyness in the trees.

3.

It was when he only called for mercy as in "God, O Take Me
Higher," while vanishing, shut up in heat, his eyes and veins
Rupturing, that I knew the night was made for many kinds of desire.

4.

Is this why they come to circle the hanging feet?
To look, to know they're looking, to be
In communion as they look, search, sway erotic.
Oh watch the freak contortions bleed to one.

5.

So I flock to these photos of the paraded dead
Like a fly to rotting: each with that inky smear that moors
The photo, though I know it is a man, was a man,
Strung up, ornament, meant to rally, as in Lord,
I done walked and done looked and done seen too much.

6.

And meant to make his human heart a heart
Set in flames, though not a sacred heart,
Parted by the lance-wound, except they had it shine.

7.

Sometimes they skinned the faces so the tongues,
When they fell, fell. Sometimes they yanked and
Hacked away, detaching limb from limb, upending.
Not Death, sometimes it was the dying that was crucial.
Seven hours once for the torture: I read this, thinking
About that body's slow unblooding union with the night.

8.

A man can die, of course, can be killed,
But can his intelligence, mind, the valley of his mind,
Which is his imagination, and extends,
Shuttles off, is nothing like the thoughtful
Knotting of a rope: a start, a middle, a definite end.

9.

Yes, a lynching knows its story best balanced
Off a tree, but a lynching can use water, Sir,
Can use stone. To burn the skin alive incites a nervous
Smell, but bullet the skin alive and get a moan.

10.

Now I understand *the eccentric to be the base*
Of design, as in this photo where the butchers
All look satisfied before the public annihilation,
Staring forward at the making of the photo, the lens.

11.

And she was there because her son was there,
Suspended, beside her. No swinging, no sway,
Their bodies like leaves kicked off the bridge's edge
High over the river that did the swaying.

12.

To look, to know you're looking, to be
Found looking at chemical and dye. If I make me
Watch these freak contortions bleed to one,
What's thought when I watch the dying?

13.

Choke every ghost with acted violence,
Stomp down the phosphorescent toes, tear off
The spittling tissues tight, you said, *tight across the bones . . .*

14.

This was the American South, American night,
The Medusa, the live head with the many tongues,
The live tongues with the many minds, and the thinking
That through a kind of swank violence and
Through a kind of steel, a beauty, a pure and crucial
History, could be found, be restored, and made endless.

15.

Between the weight and the bearing of the weight,
The final struggle and the final release,
History and the sudden knowledge of that history.

16.

Who knows the story of the pilfered god,
Osiris, unloaded and dismembered—or how his wife
Combed her imagination for his several parts,
An act of revisionist history, an act of love?
I do. This is what the boy in me knows when he decides
To enter in these photos, slowly, as into a city of snow.

17.

The sense I get from you, Emmett,
And your recanted youth,
Says that another song about you is
Just another song you didn't sing.

18.

Boneyard. Churchyard. Bloody Elysée.
Stickymarsh. Transatlantic. Place for the gone unnamed.
Potter's field. Civil War. A lump of dirt and spit.
All these brackish synonyms, huh, for death without a head.

19.

"One day, the animal expressed a doubt,
So was collared, so was ordered upstairs, and Caesar,
Who starved resistance, listened, followed, found
Himself, ropes being tied to the wrists, the block
And tackle fastened thereto, hoisted tip-toe, very
Like the day we are born: that naked and dangling."

20.

Found looking at chemical and dye, I was
My mind debating a photo. Could it kill?
Is one thought when you watch the dying
"Which is deadly: the master or his work?"

21.

When did you decide to try your endurance,
To turn back on this world dressed in a spectral night?
You know it by the ash, the wake of the crosses,
How "Shut up, Boy" burns beneath every tongue.
I wonder whose eye can resist looking back and
Not swallow them, these men: muted, gray, thinking.

22.

I know about the will, its selfishness, its entire
Greed: how it is a dark power, a moon,
And is supreme, Sir, a blue and uttermost fiction.

23.

Who is this boy that he should take these photos
And, as if into a river, slip in, fall in, am in
Complete submission, like a thumb to a mouth,
Like a thought into language, and am there,
Literally, with the hooded decade of these photos, a boy
Calling himself Isis, and I'm calling for you?

24.

To find the body a boy has to find the pieces
Of the body: the sheriff's son who got an ear, his cousin
A foot, the daughter who loves the ragged tooth,
Her souvenir, her only sanction with the dark.

25.

Again and again the melody plays, cut like a tiara.
A voice rises. "This a nigger's competence."
Cut like a tiara, the melody plays again and again.

26.

Disunion of the self develops perspective
Over strength. Your eyes may be of glass,
Sir, though your staff is a stick of blond ice.

27.

Secretly, there is a glamour here.
Not just the glamour of a human death
But death's exploitation, a bruise
Across a photo reel, a century in an instant.

28.

What will the mind do for thinking
When a body stalls, slows, diminuendos
But continue? The thinking gone on and,
Like grief, grown as pregnant as the night?
Imagine: his body, like a pendulum, a tongue,
A fever that won't break, gorgeous, that furious core.

29.

My mind debates a photo of that killed
Man, lynched man, the error between his thighs,
Which is also dead. The master's work,
I see, was to snap the penis off, control it in a jar.

30.

I have to find the mother whose snot
And crying now constitute her son,
The boy she nursed in her own arms, kissed
And sung to "Hushaby." I have to find
The father whose anger has won, who rocks
But still refuses tears in every face of weather.

31.

Blood runs the length of this body, stoic
Against the trees, stoic so that the lean of her
Head, seems, if briefly, of her desire alone. If you look
You might consider *the odd morphology of regret*,
Or instead the beauty of that lean, cocked gently, pleasure.

32.

Or this one, whose body they swung up this time
With chains, so that as he hung there the hanging
Was as much a gouging, a clawing into
The neck's plastic flesh, a breach, what art is.

33.

To negotiate the dark you must open, you must open
To the dark: dirt, the hundred worms beneath you, beneath
Where hands come to claw the dirt, let, and lay you down.

34.

The boy has found the bones, the tendons to the muscle,
The nails, the lips, both eyes, both ears.
"Osiris," he says. One heart, both feet, both thighs.
But what of that still missing stitch between the thighs?

35.

History, here is my muscle, my skin, my crucial
Blood, my heart, my stubbornness, my thinking,
My hauntedness, my ghosts, my American tongue:
I give it up. I give it all away. Here is my ending,
My making, a tableau of me traced against the night.
Take my unworthiness, my privilege. Take my hand.

36.

"Hushaby, baby, please don't you cry. Go to bed now, time for bye-bye.
When you wake, there'll be cake, and all the dream horses,
Little thunders with their eyes picked at by bees and butterflies."

37.

Man, lynched. Man, errored between the thighs,
But there was no mistake. Flesh is deliberate.
To snap the penis off, control it in a jar I see
Is to forget *mist that is golden is not wholly mist.*

38.

In the story, Isis shaped the penis out of gold.
Made of gold, the penis radiated like an ember.
An ember in Isis was a warmth in her, was a child,
Who would conquer the jealous, a dominion of blue.

39.

Who is this boy in me in need of the thing,
The needful thing that marks him "Boy"?
Did he also need *the heavy nights of drenching
Weather* to return him to his people?

40.

"And Caesar therefore became example
To all the slaving rest who did of course
Remember those awful wailing sounds
That didn't stop but only grew those nights
His master slipped the stairs to kneel,
As if a fallen god, down before him."

41.

What evidence is there for innocence at night
Among my fathers, whose nights were and still are?
Who hears but will not reckon this might be the fool
Who shuns the dark preceding him but, in shunning, will become.

42.

Lord, lift up the dark, its dry crucial
Bones. Grant me the night's insatiable thinking.
Rend me, O God, O blank tongue.

43.

Whatever I've found in their absence I've found
Repeated in me. These photos, these worked
Effigies moving like echoes, the mothers of thought.

44.

No mistake, deliberate as flesh is is the night.
Is this why they come to circle the hanging feet?
Mist that is golden is not wholly mist.
The new world communion is this: erotic.

45.

In the story, Isis shaped the penis out of mud.
Made of mud, the penis rounded inside.
A circle in Isis was a world in Isis, was a love,
That would travel the mind, an eye for every idea.

46.

The camera positions:
Between the weight and the bearing of the weight.
The camera questions:
The final struggle and the final release.
The camera makes a choice:
History and the sudden knowledge of that history.

47.

That quick incision. A cut. Close but not
Too close to the base. Swift, and with a fist
Pressed down, to prevent the blood—.
So the boy's penis unlocks like a votive door in which leaves
Fly out, falling, and, historical, also having fallen.

48.

Dance for me, starlight, in the skittish whips of the water.
I'm bleeding. Glint for me, aperture in the sky.
Kiss me deeply, deeply, the one I've resurrected. Sing as you rise.

49.

They are like bronze statues emblazoned
Like squares of metal; like sure men
Emboldened and dipped in oil; like confessions
Whispered at the longest tables: these bones that build a canon.

50.

The trees are seeking something more than blood
To shine with. A street has now been likened
To a tree. What number of hands, together, can wash it clear?
But my hands move to bring that color closer to your lips.

Crescendo

But I'm trying hard to know what
is meant when we claim *O silent night*—
a night like this, when blown out is all
the blaze of the sky but not heat, not
dampness either, not even that star, alone,
like a crack in the firmament (*in the levees*)
and what floods in, because only it can,
is a light to make light of till we can't—
then a breeze passes, with its humanlike
moan: since it's human I can know it, I hear it,
as I do the magnolia-shudder, the bird
-scatter, as I do the river: can't you hear it
singing far off—?
                            Then not as far—?

Undiscovered Genius of the Mississippi Delta

Jean-Michel Basquiat, late twentieth century,
acrylic, oilstick, and paper collage on canvas

Loss is not something
      worth worrying over, if
truly loss

                This

                    is the song

      ◆

So we see here this
      river making away
itself, perverting   *we've always known*
      to its many tangents—
Are not sad

      ◆

The genius might be
      to remain unfound,   *Mississippi*
unfounded,
      outside the reach of the West,   *Mississippi*
for as long as one can . . .

      ◆

Maybe the river is a boy   *This*
      ankle-deep in the mud,
his face arced over   *is the song*
      the water brown enough
so that he saw himself

      ◆

Who was designed a slave,
            beast of burden, he says
he was—that his blood and sweat, oh
            every inch is   *Finally*
this Republican land

            ◆

The genius might be
            that he was still unsatisfied,   *we've reached*
would not be set—
            but lay there in the middle of things,
uncombined

            ◆

So he's been sinking then
            this whole time, his whole   *the end*
body consumed
            by that mud—till what remained: a figure,
the singing, singular head . . .

                                        of narrative

Study in Black

Tu Fu, "Thoughts While Traveling at Night"

There's a wind in the grass—
Is there here
    a boat's mast claiming my lonely night too?
                                 I see the stars
       can't be called *hanged*, exactly,
just *hanging down*,
                not over emptiness, but honest ground,
the moon trying the black skin of this river, black corpse . . .
                              But, even plainer—
    I wonder if these words, my words,
will ever bring me fame.
    I have my age, my injuries. They limit me.
                          I'm like some spook bird
I know, solo and roped between
                  where rotting happens and a sky.

A Southern Wind

Quiet as a seed, and as guarded,
our walking took the shape of two people
uneasy together. I had the feeling
that on the anxious incline of that hill we gave the hill
one reason for being. What loneliness, what
privacy was in that? *Hey,* I said. *Race me to the top?*
Then is when I nearly tripped on the sly earth,
an earth shaping to itself again. A stone?
But, no, picking it up, bringing the wormed-through
black flesh of it to my height, I knew it for
an apple and gnashed and let the juices freak and down
my face. Don't ask me why I did it. I know.
I know there are poisons like these we have
to feed each other, promises we try to hold—though
how can they be contained? I wanted to give you
what I could of me. To be personal, without
confession. I wanted to believe in the constancy of that hill.
Daylight was tiring. The air, secret, alone.
I won, you said. *You did,* I said. So we stood there.

This Pair This Marriage of Two

Half-naked fevering standing
Up with a feather inked until it bled

Just above newly above the

Collarbone near the neck curved
There an apostrophe

Am I what that is that

Surface ekphrastic wrong to touch *But*
Touch me it begs so I try it extend a finger

Toward no real success

Must it be true
That everything I make will be a self

Eulogy for what it fails to be

A set of lines across the skin even
This dusky reflection I am myself looking

At this picture of myself made

Of metal and light light and glass it's there
I can see its strictness I can see

My eyes as ever haunted as the letter

O they are defining me this pair this marriage
Of two hollow suns but charged but

Can't a space be charged

With accent what creeps outside the
Visible what I see inside the mirror is it maybe

What I can't see what instead

I've been made to perceive
That voice colonial scribbled in wrong

Color twisted tones *You're such*

A problem child Whiten yourself
Straighten

Your speech but could it be

That what terrifies first is not
The image in the mirror but is the mirror

Fact that I can at all be

Reflected can be made to be seen and deeper
Than what I've been taught depth is

When I wrote

"I'm trying to write obsession into it" I meant
That deepness a reach toward a dead

Loss an understood failure

As when I had them scratch this dumb
Feather into my skin (*death, which is birds lifting*)

This feather I'm at pain

To touch as if communion were
True as if my body were honestly true I was saying

I myself am

Too heavy am a screen too scored to lift up
But try it

I think there might be pleasure

In this in failure might be a need for it
Is that why I'd stare at a burning cross two men

Burning at the edge of a field

Is that why when they're absent I invent them
Is that why I'm here

Companied with a surface an echo

Of myself locked an X
I make and I make and I make

"Do not imagine

You can abdicate" a teacher once said
But to imagine sir

To imagine is the one mirror I trust

Do You Feel Me?

First, wild lotus on the surface
of blue water, the great
blue heron striking the ways.
I need to find myself, I told myself.
To live the limits of this body.

Then, I invented "you."
Like a bridge between two distances,
you guided me: here, fields
of the expansive, wild clover.
My hands, my feet. There,

fields of gray water. You
who increasingly made me
conscious of myself, continue.
Listen to me when I say
I will cross into Jordan.

Swamp lilies in the camplight,
the moonlight opening like a kiss.
This is what happens when
any two things meet: some water,
a city enveloped, blue—.

How each becomes the revelation
of what the other can do.

Mood for Love

1.

(*There I go.*) I am the man
stepping up to the water. I am not
the man I leave behind,
his arms snapped before him (*at me*)—
taut as when a whip means
giddyup, move. Yes, my knees
are trembling, like water remembering . . .
I suffer, I am that man ready to quit.
Should I turn back will I face—?
Should I turn back—?
Should I turn back will I have to face
his palms (*they are your palms*)
open, and pushing me to the river?
Will I hear them cry *Have faith?*

2.

In the story, Jesus follows
the fishermen after he tells the fishermen
to sail ahead. Yes, he's anointed.
Yes, he's blessed. But what matters
are his eyes, fixed on the fishermen.
Then begins his walking mystery.
No injury. Each step a step toward
the brotherhood there in that boat in the lake.
It's as if each step is carried by
that brotherhood rough in the lake.
He's hardly wet as they drag him in,
those fishermen, except as he kisses
each of them and they, devoted
(*thunderstruck*), kiss him back.

3.

(*There I go.*) I am the man
stepping onto the water (*in the story,*
water simply obeys) because
you've told me so, told me the duties
of the struck-in-love (*as my soul*
as I go will obey). Here is our house.
Here is the hole in the roof from where
we escaped our house (*the water rising*).
Here on this roof: I look out at the river expanded.
(*I suffer, I'm that man anonymous in the waves.*)
We need food. (*I was there.*) We need water.
(*There I go.*) I am the man stepping onto
the sick water (*let it obey*). And you are the man
who follows.

Faggot

As when a word lifts unexpectedly
                         or implodes—
you had meant to say *maelstrom* but now
interposed between you and the open world,
male-storm (no one would think to give a sex
to it, so were unready)—that was its arrival,

                                       fire
that didn't act as one sheet but gathered
separately as flames around some common matter:
call it a heart, make this a Catholic scene, only the thorns
are missing unless they lie, like everything else,
beneath this oil-slicked water now risen, now ignited, as we are
ignited—like faggots thrown at the sinner's feet
as he shakes, as he shouts *It was only for love*, as when all words abandon . . .

You Are Not Christ

For the drowning, yes, there is always panic.
Or peace. Your body behaving finally by instinct
alone. Crossing out wonder. Crossing out
a need to know. You only feel you need to live.
That you deserve it. Even here. Even as your chest
fills with a strange new air, you will not ask
what this means. Like prey caught in the wolf's teeth,
but you are not the lamb. You are what's in the lamb
that keeps it kicking. Let it.

No Ararat

Is true. I was there. The city wrestled. The radio said this could be the one. We gathered. I held on to my mother's hand. I held on to my mother holding her mother's hand. I didn't dream this. Awful hollering. I slept through that hollering. Wind in awe of earth. I woke up. *You might as well go back*, my grandmother said. *You done slept through most of it.* I woke up. She was laughing. *Oh, you should've seen it!* It was morning. *No sooner did he put head to pillow, Uncle Vernon shot up, hollering, "The roof! Damn storm done ate the roof!"* I didn't dream this. There was a storm. Then there wasn't. The day after came like a hammer through glass. The sky shook off his clothes and was brilliant. I tell you it was necessary: violence had to preface such beauty. I saw the down trees, the down power lines, and broken glass. I saw the life I once had rise from me like a tiny balloon. In the distance, the Dome. Bright. White as a burning eye. It had the permanency of a mountain—as where Noah landed. *My God*, I whispered. The radio said there is no god.

Epitaph on a Stone

Like you, I was born underwater.
(*I lied: there was never a stone.*)
Like you, I was born but that's not the half of it:
I lived. Lord, I lived. Like a cancer, I crept
sideways. Like a scorpion, I lied. I lived
the way a problem lives, openly, so much
earth wanted me closed. Don't you know the dead
are not easy? Don't you know they crave?
I stepped out of the water (*I was made doing this*) slick-
skinned, fluent, a character: my eyes twice
haunted, my humor, my voice—and can't you hear
shackles running the length of my voice? I was born
in a minute, in a panic, on a whim. A mistake,
I mean. A choice between this world and a body,
pretty fault where a heart should be.

Black Gentleman

O fly away home fly away . . .

— Robert Hayden

There are eyes, glasses even, but still he can't see
    what the world sees seeing him.
They know an image of him they themselves created.
He knows his own: fine-lined from foot to finger,
each limb adjusted, because it's had to,
    to achieve finally flight—

        though what's believed
in him is a flightlessness, a sinking-down,
as any swamp-mess of water I'm always thinking of
might draw down again the washed-up body
of a boy, as any mouth I've yearned for would take down,
wrestler-style, the boy's tongue with its own . . .

        What an eye can't imagine
it can't find: not in blood, swollen in the stiff knees
of a cypress, not definitely in some dreaming man's dream—.
    Let's have his nature speak.
What will the incredible night of him say here, to his thousand
moons, now that he can rise up to any tree, rope or none, but not fear it?

Take it Easy

That the light stalks your skin,
no, that your skin makes it: a radiating
hum, jive, a freedom, a beehive
packed just as much with honey as does it
hazard; also, a balm for where the sting sits,
a treaty, country upon which I first
laid my claim, but was usurped; where
carefully do I move to cross it again. Now here
come my lips to it, pink over your body's
good bark. Now here is my mouth, entire.
I'm scared of you, baby, it says, scared like a god
is of his faithful—and like the faithful. Light
-struck. Delighted. Terrorstruck. Come, lift up
your gates, your countenance spread like a lily upon me:
whip me, I am so whipped. These are my eyes.

Boy with Thorn

Unknown, first century BC, bronze

1.

Entered, those shadows spoke his loneliness
like a god.

2.

This was new knowledge. The kind he had little
business knowing. The mere
    risk of it making it
all the more delicious.

3.

A forced-out confession. A forcing-it-in.

4.

Each push, where the blood yawned like an opiate.
Each inch, a hermeneutics of the self.

5.

Would you feed on such hurting, would you drink so much?

6.

Was he so terrible a thing to look at?
But was looked at.

7.

His face chiseled deliberate.
His face, a question gone unanswered—

8.

There could have been a thorn already inside? His tongue.
Scratching its wrongs, speaking its six troubles.

9.

How?

10.

There could have been a thorn already inside? The point in his eye.
What makes the shadows their acutest when they lift and sprawl.

11.

I keep thinking of the thorn as
a marker, scrawler, what shapes the places both excused
    and forbidden
in his body's swamp.

12.

Violence thou shalt want. Violence thou shalt steal
and store inside.

13.

This Spinario, Fedele, boy with
a message, a mission; Pickaninny—
    Who would not stop for
damage, the old story goes . . .

14.

Shame, guilt, spleen, woe, shock, and want.

15.

He wanted them gone, I know: all his deeper hurts,
poorer gods, that lush resentment.

16.

But failed. They were greater dark, vials of
mystery, done things.

17.

Take it. Don't you have to learn
to take it, eventually?

18.

I told him the thorn was as a key,
his body a lock.

19.

I made him meet the key up with the lock. Turn.

20.

I told him, *Rickey, turn—*

21.

He did: an anti-chrysalis, a lyric,
which is the piece of a prayer visible.

22.

Until he rewound: a new republic, a kingdom where not savagely
he was king.

23.

Who could bare the wind?

24.

Who could feel the self demanding the self?

25.

Who could see his honesty? His face more handsome
once the pain combed
    through, combed like a river
too clean for love.

26.

*Violence thou shalt want. Violence thou shalt steal
and store inside.*

27.

He would devour it.

28.

This was his body, his body
finally his.

29.

He shut the thorn up in his foot, and told his foot
Walk.

NOTES

The epigraph is from W. H. Auden's poem "The Question" (1930), from his *Collected Poems*, edited by Edward Mendelson.

◆

"I Saw I Dreamt Two Men" alludes, in part, to the series of "Anti-Homosexuality" or "Kill the Gays" bills that have been proposed in several African nations since 2000, often with support from U.S. conservative Christian organizations and ministers, such as Scott Lively. These acts of legislation moved to broaden the criminalization of homosexuality, sometimes with punishments up to death.

◆

"Black Iris" was occasioned by the painting *Black Iris III*, by Georgia O'Keeffe. This painting also inspires the last table setting in Judy Chicago's *The Dinner Party*, which memorializes over a thousand women in history and is installed permanently at the Brooklyn Museum.

◆

Vanitas with Negro Boy, by David Bailly, follows in the tradition of vanitas paintings by making reference to human mortality through still life representations of various ephemera, such as burning candles, decaying flowers, or even human skulls. This painting by Bailly also depicts, most interestingly, a man (possibly a servant) of noticeable

African or Moorish descent holding between his thumb and index finger a small mini-portrait of the head of the man who, some have argued, was likely the European patron who commissioned the painting. Installed today as a part of the permanent collection at Herbert F. Johnson Museum of Art at Cornell University, the painting's title also holds historical interest: in an exhibition in 1991, the title was listed as *Vanitas with Negro Boy*; however, in an exhibition just a few years later, in 1998, the title was revised as *Vanitas Still Life with Portrait*.

◆

"Little Song" is scaffolded, as the line endings reveal, around a line lifted from Robert Duncan's poem "Passages 18: The Torso."

◆

"He who Refuses Does Not Repent" derives its title from a line from "Che Fece . . . Il Gran Refiuto," by C. P. Cavafy, as translated by Edmund Keeley and Phillip Sherrard.

◆

Throughout "Of the Leaves That Have Fallen," all italicized text is lifted directly from Stevens's "Like Decorations in a Nigger Cemetery." This poem owes a debt to *Without Sanctuary: Lynching Photography in America*, edited by James Allen; *The Black Book*, edited by Middleton A. Harris; and several essays by James Baldwin, especially "Stranger in the Village," and "Nobody Knows My Name," where the notion of the night being made for desire can be found.

◆

Undiscovered Genius of the Mississippi Delta, by Jean-Michel Basquiat, is installed as a part of the Nicola Erni Collection in Steinhausen, Switzerland. Read as his racial history of America, specifically the Deep South, Basquiat completed the painting, which extends over several joined canvases, in 1983; however, it wouldn't be until 1988 when he, with Outtarra Watts, beheld the river at its fullest when the two traveled to New Orleans for the city's annual Jazz and Heritage Festival. Though it's said Basquiat was enchanted by the city, no doubt for its deeply Afro-Atlantic sensibilities, that trip would be the only occasion Basquiat visited New Orleans. He died on August 12, 1988, about six months before the author's birthday.

◆

"This Pair This Marriage of Two" quotes at its conclusion a line by W. H. Auden from his poem "Venus Will Now Say a Few Words," from his *Collected Poems*, edited by Edward Mendelson.

◆

The dome referenced in "No Ararat" refers to the Louisiana Superdome, which housed approximately 26,000 people as a "shelter of last resort" for those unable to evacuate the city for Hurricane Katrina. The hurricane made landfall in Louisiana on the morning of Monday, August 29. 2005. Its strom surge led to fifty-three different levee breaches, causing significant flooding of up to fifteen feet throughout the city. For days after, federal relief was slow to rescue deserted survivors.

◆

The epigraph to "Black Gentleman" comes from Robert Hayden's "O Daedalus, Fly Away Home," from his *Collected Poems*, edited by Frederick Glaysher.

◆

"Boy with Thorn" meditates on an ancient Greco-Roman sculpture depicting an adolescent boy withdrawing a thorn from the sole of his foot. The work is one of few to survive antiquity due to heavy reproduction and copying throughout the centuries. Various chronological dates have been proposed for its exact date of origin, spanning the third to first century, but a date after 50 BC can be assumed based on stylistic features of the face and hair. Several centuries later the caricature of the pickaninny was invented, who was a black juvenile figure that, at least as argued by Robin Bernstein, was "always resistant, if not immune, to pain." Are we sure?

ACKNOWLEDGMENTS

My thanks to the editors of the various journals where some of these poems, often in earlier versions, first appeared:

Anti-: "Epitaph on a Stone" (as "Epitaph at the Foot of the Stone"), "Quiet Please"; *Boston Review*: "Of the Leaves That Have Fallen," "Undiscovered Genius of the Mississippi Delta"; *Callaloo*: "Conditions for a Southern Gothic," "Do You Feel Me?," "This Pair This Marriage Of Two" (as "Late Meditation"), "One Country"; *The Collagist*: "You Are Not Christ"; *Diagram*: "Full"; *Feminist Wire*: "Mood for Love," "Take it Easy"; *Fence*: "Boy with Thorn," "He who Refuses Does Not Repent"; *Ganymede Unfinished*: "Mood Indigo"; *jubilat*: "Crescendo"; *Knockout Literary Magazine*: "Faggot," "Modern Ripple"; *Linebreak*: "No Ararat"; *Maggy*: "King of Shade, King of Scorpions"; *Muzzle*: "Carnal Knowledge"; *Other Journal*: "Ghazal for Emmett Till"; *Oxford American*: "Little Song"; *Paris-American*: "A Southern Wind," "Vanitas with Negro Boy"; *Poetry*: "Black Gentleman," "I Saw I Dreamt Two Men," "Southern Gothic," "Study in Black," "Swing Low," "Writing an Elegy"; *Vinyl*: "Black Iris."

◆

"No Ararat," "Black Gentleman," and "Southern Gothic" were translated into Spanish for *Tierra Adentro Magazine* (Mexico).

◆

"No Ararat," "Crescendo," "One Country," and "Take it Easy" have also been translated into Ukrainian for a forthcoming anthology of young American poetry.

◆

"Lord and Chariot" was reprinted in *Poetry Daily*.

◆

"Mood Indigo" was reprinted in *Pank*.

◆

"You Are Not Christ" was reprinted in *Poetry*.

◆

"Swing Low" was reprinted in *The New York Times (T Magazine)*.

◆

Excerpts from "Of the Leaves That Have Fallen" were published in *Extraordinary Rendition: (American) Writers Speak of Palestine*, edited by Ru Freeman.

◆

Finally, some of these poems also appeared in the chapbooks, *Whipped*, published by Floating Wolf Quarterly, and *Prime*, published by Sibling Rivalry Press.

◆

My deepest gratitude also extends to the following institutions who helped or granted me the time, space, inspiration, or funds necessary to construct these poems: the Atlantic Center for the Arts, the Bread Loaf Writer's Conference, Cave Canem Foundation, the Civitella Ranieri Foundation in Italy, the National Endowment for the Arts, Poetry Foundation, Prospect.3 New Orleans, Sarah Lawrence College, Washington University in St Louis, and the Virginia Center for the Creative Arts. My love and appreciation reach far and wide, but especially the following individuals—mentors, teachers, friends, and family alike—always for their degrees of light and shade: Robert M. Whitehead, Phillip B. Williams, L. Lamar Wilson, Caitlin Tyler, Nicole Sealey, Solmaz Sharif, Emilyn Sosa, Javier Stevens, Roger Reeves, Miriam Pace, Carl Phillips, Rowan Ricardo Phillips, Dante Micheaux, John Murillo, Eileen Myles, Chaun Lewis, Glenn Ligon, John Keene, A. Van Jordan, Matthea Harvey, Cathy Park Hong, Suzanne Gardinier, Rachel Eliza Griffiths, Sara Gonzalez, Timothy Donnelly, Mary Jo Bang, Jericho Brown, Julie Abraham, Neil Arditi, my loving family on South Galvez Street, especially my mother, and, of course, Terrance Hayes.

◆

I dedicate this book to the memory of my grandfather, who read to me.